MERRY
Christmas

WOULD YOU RATHER

HAVE A PUMPKIN PIE FIGHT

OR

AN APPLE PIE FIGHT WITH FRIENDS?

WOULD YOU RATHER

HAVE ELF EARS

········· OR ·········

A SANTA BEARD?

WOULD YOU RATHER

HAVE RUDOLF FOLLOW YOU AROUND EVERY DAY UNTIL CHRISTMAS

· · · · · · · · · · · · · OR · · · · · · · · · · · · ·

BE FOLLOWED BY FROSTY THE SNOWMAN?

WOULD YOU RATHER

WRAP CHRISTMAS PRESENTS FOR 8 HOURS

····················· OR ·····················

HELP CHILDREN TAKE PICTURES WITH SANTA AT THE MALL?

7 HOURS OF CHRISTMAS SHOPPING

············· OR ·············

10 HOURS OF CHRISTMAS MOVIES?

WOULD YOU RATHER

HAVE A RED RUDOLF NOSE

········· OR ·········

A FROSTY BUTTON NOSE?

WOULD YOU RATHER

ASK EVERYONE YOU MEET THEIR FAVORITE COLOR

· · · · · · · · · · · · · · · · · OR · · · · · · · · · · · · · · ·

SMILE REALLY BIG AT EVERYONE AND NOT SAY ANYTHING?

WOULD YOU RATHER

MAKE SNOW ANGELS

························ OR ·····················

GO ICE SKATING?

LIVE IN A GIANT GINGERBREAD HOUSE

······· OR ·······

IN SANTA'S TOY SHOP?

WOULD YOU RATHER

EAT ONLY FRUITCAKE FOR A WEEK

······· OR ·······

DRINK ONLY EGG NOG FOR A WEEK?

7 LEVELS OF THE CANDY CANE FOREST

···································· **OR** ························

SEA OF SWIRLY WHIRLY GUMDROPS?

WOULD YOU RATHER

HAVE CANDY CANE LEGS

· · · · · · · · · · · · · · · OR · · · · · · · · · · · · · · ·

GUM DROPS FOR EYES

WOULD YOU RATHER

SING JINGLE BELLS
ONCE EVERY HOUR FOR 2
WEEKS

······ OR ······

WEAR AN ELF
COSTUME
TO SCHOOL FOR 1 WEEK?

WOULD YOU RATHER

WEAR A HAT MADE OF MISTLETOE

OR

WEAR JINGLE BELLS ON YOUR FEET FOR A WEEK?

WOULD YOU RATHER

HAVE MITTENS FOR HANDS

····· OR ·····

HAVE SKI'S FOR FEET?

WOULD YOU RATHER

HAVE YOUR ELF ON A SHELF TALK TO YOU

·········· OR ··········

TALK WITH YOUR CHRISTMAS TREE?

WOULD YOU RATHER

BE HOME WITH FAMILY FOR THE HOLIDAYS

• • • • • • • • • • • • • • • OR • • • • • • • • • • • • • •

GO DISNEYWORLD BY YOURSELF?

WOULD YOU RATHER

SING CHRISTMAS
CARROLS BY YOURSELF

········· **OR** ·········

SIT ON SANTA'S LAP
FOR 1 HOUR?

WOULD YOU RATHER

RAKE LEAVES

OR

SHOVEL SNOW?

WOULD YOU RATHER

BE AN ELF AT THE
NORTH POLE

· · · · · · · · · · · · · OR · · · · · · · · · · · · ·

ONE OF SANTA'S
REINDEER?

HAVE EYES MADE OUT OF COAL

························· OR ·····················

REINDEER FEET?

WOULD YOU RATHER

BE SNOWED IN WITH LOTS OF FAMILY DURING THE HOLIDAYS

OR

ON A BEACH WITH JUST A FEW OF YOUR FAMILY?

WOULD YOU RATHER

SPEND 11 HOURS UNTANGLING CHRISTMAS LIGHTS

·········· OR ··········

FIND THE ONE LIGHT THAT IS OUT ON A STRING OF CHRISTMAS LIGHTS A MILE LONG?

DO BONFIRE AND SMORES

···············OR···············

WATCH HOLIDAY VIDEO AND DRINK HOT CHOCOLATE?

BE AN ANGEL ON TOP OF THE TREE

OR

A JACK IN THE BOX TOY?

SPEND A DAY WITH
THE GRINCH

· · · · · · · · · · · · · · · OR · · · · · · · · · · · · · · ·

JACK FROST?

WOULD YOU RATHER

GO SLEDDING

·········· OR ··········

TAKE A HORSE DRAWN SLEIGH RIDE?

WOULD YOU RATHER

WRAP 100 PRESENTS

················· **OR** ··············

DECORATE 10 TREES?

WOULD YOU RATHER

HAVE HOLLY FOR HAIR

· · · · · · · · · · · · · · · · · · · **OR** · · · · · · · · · · · · · · · · · ·

WEAR CHRISTMAS STOCKINGS FOR LEGS?

WEAR UGLY CHRISTMAS SWEATERS FOR 1 YEAR

OR

STAY WITH THE ABDOMINAL SNOWMAN FOR 1 WEEK?

WOULD YOU RATHER

TAKE A LOOK AT SANTA'S LIST

OR

PEEK AT YOUR PRESENTS?

WOULD YOU RATHER

LAUGH LIKE SANTA

OR

TALK LIKE AN ELF?

STRING A MILE OR POPCORN GARLAND

············ **OR** ············

LIGHT & KEEP 500 CANDLES BURNING AT ONCE?

NEVER EAT CANDY AGAIN

OR

NEVER PLAY IN THE SNOW AGAIN?

WOULD YOU RATHER

YOUR HAIR ALWAYS
SMELL LIKE
TURKEY

· · · · · · · · · · · · · · · OR · · · · · · · · · · · · · · ·

CHIMNEY SMOKE?

WOULD YOU RATHER

NEVER HAVE HOT CHOCOLATE AGAIN

········· OR ··········

NEVER WATCH A CHRISTMAS MOVIE EVER AGAIN?

WOULD YOU RATHER

SIT IN A TUB OF HOT
CHOCOLATE
FOR 6 HOURS

······· OR ·······

TRY TO STUFF 100
MARSHMALLOWS IN
YOUR MOUTH?

WOULD YOU RATHER

ONLY BE ABLE TO SPEAK IN CHRISTMAS SONG LYRICS

OR

ONLY BE ABLE TO SPEAK IN CHRISTMAS MOVIE QUOTES?

WOULD YOU RATHER

HAVE HOLIDAY DECORATIONS UP ALL YEAR

········· OR ·········

NEVER BE ABLE TO PUT THEM UP AGAIN?

HAVE SANTA CLAUS
SNEEZE
IN YOUR FACE

· · · · · · · · · · · · · OR · · · · · · · · · · · · ·

HAVE A REINDEER POOP
ON YOUR SHOES?

WOULD YOU RATHER

SING CHRISTMAS SONGS
SOLO TO AN AUDIENCE
OF 2 MILLION PEOPLE

········· OR ·········

WET YOUR PANTS WHILE
SITTING ON
SANTA'S LAP?

WOULD YOU RATHER

HAVE A BIG BELLY LIKE
SANTA CLAUS

·············· OR ··············

HAVE A BIG GLOWING
RED NOSE
LIKE RUDOLPH?

WOULD YOU RATHER

BE COMPLETELY ALONE

····················· OR ·····················

HAVE 100 PEOPLE CRAMMED INTO YOUR HOUSE ALL CHRISTMAS DAY?

BE PERMANENTLY COVERED HEAD TO TOE IN FUR

· · · · · · · · · · · · · **OR** · · · · · · · · · · · · · ·

HAVE ANTLERS THAT FALL OFF AND GROW BACK EVERY YEAR?

HAVE A CARROT FOR A NOSE

············ **OR** ············

REINDEER HOOF HANDS?

HAVE 'HO HO HO!' AS YOUR USUAL LAUGH

OR

HAVE A HIGH SQUEAKY VOICE LIKE AN ELF?

WOULD YOU RATHER

BE THE ONLY PERSON TO NOT RECEIVE A GIFT

······ **OR** ······

BE THE ONLY PERSON THAT GAVE GIFTS?

HAVE A TALKING
CHRISTMAS TREE
THAT
NEVER STOPS TALKING
ABOUT TREE STUFF

········· OR ·········

HAVE A LIT
FIREPLACE THAT NEVER
GOES OUT?

WOULD YOU RATHER

GET STUCK IN A
CHIMNEY
FOR FOUR HOURS

·············· OR ··············

WEAR A DIFFERENT
UGLY
CHRISTMAS SWEATER

EVERY DAY
FOR FOUR MONTHS?

WOULD YOU RATHER

DECORATE AN 80-FT TALL GINGERBREAD MAN

OR

BAKE A 1-TON FRUITCAKE?

WEAR SANTA'S RED SUIT TO SCHOOL

OR

A GREEN ELF SUIT TO SCHOOL?

WOULD YOU RATHER

BE BEST
FRIENDS WITH FROSTY
THE SNOWMAN

······· OR ···············

RUDOLPH THE RED NOSED
REINDEER ?

WOULD YOU RATHER

RECEIVE ONE BIG PRESENT

· · · · · · · · · · · · · · · OR · · · · · · · · · · · · · · ·

10 SMALL PRESENTS?

WOULD YOU RATHER

OPEN YOUR PRESENTS
ON CHRISTMAS EVE

· · · · · · · · · · · · · · · OR · · · · · · · · · · · ·

ON CHRISTMAS
MORNING?

EAT CHRISTMAS
COOKIES FOR 6 MONTH

· · · · · · · · · · · · · OR · · · · · · · · · · · · ·

EAT CANDY CANES FOR
6 MONTHS?

BE A MOUSE AND
RECEIVE A BIG PIECE OF
CHEESE
FOR CHRISTMAS

. . . . OR . . . .

NEVER BE ABLE TO
PUT THEM UP AGAIN?

WEAR SANTA'S BIG BOOTS TO GYM CLASS

········· **OR** ·········

WEAR POINTY ELF SHOES?

BE MRS. CLAUS

······· OR ···········

BE THE HEAD ELF IN
SANTA'S WORKSHOP?

WOULD YOU RATHER

LIVE AT THE NORTH POLE

········· **OR** ·········

LIVE AT THE SOUTH POLE?

EAT A GINGERBREAD HOUSE

···· OR ····

LIVE IN A GINGERBREAD HOUSE?

WOULD YOU RATHER

HAVE A BELLY THAT
SHAKES LIKE A
BOWL FULL OF JELLY

························· OR ··············

EAT A BOWL FULL OF
JELLY?

WOULD YOU RATHER

BE A MELTING SNOWMAN

············ OR ············

MUNCHED ON
GINGERBREAD PERSON?

WOULD YOU RATHER

MAKE TOYS ALL YEAR LONG

······· OR ·······

PLAY WITH TOYS ALL YEAR LONG?

WOULD YOU RATHER

EAT CHRISTMAS COOKIES WITH SANTA

············· OR ·············

BAKE CHRISTMAS COOKIES WITH SANTA?

WOULD YOU RATHER

VISIT THE NORTH POLE

····················· OR ·····················

VISIT DISNEY WORLD?

WOULD YOU RATHER

HAVE A HALLOWEEN PARTY

OR

HAVE A CHRISTMAS PARTY?

WOULD YOU RATHER

DRIVE A SLEIGH

· · · · · · · · · · · · · · OR · · · · · · · · · · · · · ·

RIDE ON A REINDEER?

WOULD YOU RATHER

MAKE
TOYS IN THE WORKSHOP

OR

DELIVER TOYS ALL
OVER
THE WORLD?

WOULD YOU RATHER

LISTEN
TO ONLY CHRISTMAS
MUSIC FOR A WEEK

······· OR ·······

SING ONLY CHRISTMAS
SONGS FOR A WEEK?

WOULD YOU RATHER

GO ICE SKATING

• • • • • • • • • • • • • • • • • OR • • • • • • • • • • • • • • • • •

GO SNOWBOARDING?

WOULD YOU RATHER

SMELL LIKE A PINE TREE

· · · · · · · · · · · · · OR · · · · · · · · · · · · ·

LOOK LIKE A GINGERBREAD MAN/WOMAN?

TRAIN THE REINDEER

···OR···

BE THE HEAD ELF?

MEET THE GRINCH

OR

SHOVEL SNOW FOR 5 HOURS?

WOULD YOU RATHER

MAKE A GINGERBREAD HOUSE

······· OR ·······

OPEN ONE CHRISTMAS GIFT A DAY EARLY?

MAKE A SNOW FORT

········· OR ·········

HAVE A SNOWBALL FIGHT?

SHOP FOR GIFTS THE DAY BEFORE CHRISTMAS

.... **OR** ....

SHOP FOR CHRISTMAS GIFTS ALL YEAR LONG?

JUMP IN THE WORLD'S BIGGEST PILE OF SNOW

· · · · · · · · · · · · · OR · · · · · · · · · · · · ·

SKI DOWN THE BIGGEST MOUNTAIN IN THE WORLD?

WOULD YOU RATHER

HAVE EVERYTHING YOU
TOUCH CRUMBLE
AND
FALL APART LIKE SNOW

·············· OR ··············

HAVE EVERYTHING YOU
TOUCH
TURN TO SOLID ICE?

HAVE A SNOWY AND COLD CHRISTMAS

• • • • • • • • • • • • • OR • • • • • • • • • • • • •

HAVE A WARM CHRISTMAS WITH NO SNOW?

LIVE IN THE WORLD'S
FANCIEST
ICE PALACE

· · · · · · · · · · · · · · OR · · · · · · · · · · · · ·

LIVE IN THE WORLD'S
LARGEST IGLOO?

WOULD YOU RATHER

CELEBRATE CHRISTMAS
2 TIMES PER YEAR

······· OR ·······

CELEBRATE YOUR
BIRTHDAY
2 TIMES PER YEAR?

HAVE OLAF FOR A FRIEND

······· OR ···········

HAVE ELSA FOR A FRIEND?

WOULD YOU RATHER

BE ABLE TO TRAVEL
THE WORLD IN ONE NIGHT

·············· OR ··············

BE ABLE TO CREATE
ANYTHING YOU WANT
OUT OF ICE?

BE A POLAR BEAR

· · · · · · · · · · · · · · · · · **OR** · · · · · · · · · · · · · · ·

BE A PENGUIN?

WOULD YOU RATHER

STICK YOUR HAND IN A BUCKET OF ICE WATER

OR

STICK YOUR FACE IN A PILE OF SNOW?

SPEND ALL DAY WATCHING CHRISTMAS MOVIES

OR

SPEND ALL DAY SLEDDING?

STRING A
MILE-LONG
POPCORN GARLAND

······· OR ·······

LIGHT 500 CANDLES?

WOULD YOU RATHER

GO SHOPPING ON BLACK FRIDAY

OR

GO SHOPPING ON CHRISTMAS EVE?

WOULD YOU RATHER

HAVE ALL WHITE TREE LIGHTS

·············· OR ··············

COLORFUL TREE LIGHTS?

WOULD YOU RATHER

HAVE A CHRISTMAS SWEATER THAT LIGHTS UP

············ OR ············

A CHRISTMAS SWEATER THAT SINGS?

WOULD YOU RATHER

HAVE YOUR BIRTHDAY
BE ON CHRISTMAS

············ OR ···············

SHARE YOUR BIRTHDAY
WITH YOUR BROTHERS
AND SISTERS?

WOULD YOU RATHER

SPEND CHRISTMAS WITH YOUR FAVORITE MOVIE CHARACTER

········· OR ·········

YOUR FAVORITE TV CHARACTER?

WOULD YOU RATHER

HAVE COOKIES AND MILK LEFT OUT IF YOU WERE SANTA CLAUS

················· OR ··············

PIZZA AND COKE?

EAT ONLY HOLIDAY FOOD

OR

WATCH ONLY HOLIDAY MOVIES?

WOULD YOU RATHER

HAVE A HOLIDAY PARTY EVERY NIGHT

······· OR ·······

HAVE NO HOLIDAY PARTIES TO ATTEND?

HAVE ALL YOUR PRESENTS WRAPPED TERRIBLY

········· OR ·········

NOT HAVE THEM WRAPPED AT ALL?

WOULD YOU RATHER

HAVE AN ENTIRE SNOW WEEK OFF FROM SCHOOL

···················· OR ··················

HAVE AN EXTRA WEEK OF SUMMER VACATION?

WOULD YOU RATHER

WEAR A CHRISTMAS JUMPER

OR

A SANTA HAT?

WOULD YOU RATHER

HAVE CHRISTMAS EVERY DAY

· · · · · · · · · · · OR · · · · · · · · · · ·

YOUR BIRTHDAY EVERY DAY?

WOULD YOU RATHER

BE SURPRISED BY
YOUR
CHRISTMAS PRESENTS

· · · · · · · · · · · · · OR · · · · · · · · · · · · · ·

KNOW ALL YOUR
CHRISTMAS PRESENTS?

Made in the USA
Coppell, TX
08 October 2021